EASY POP MELODIES
FOR VIOLIN

ISBN 978-1-4803-8435-4

HAL•LEONARD®
CORPORATION

7777 W. BLUEMOUND RD. P.O. BOX 13819 MILWAUKEE, WI 53213

Visit Hal Leonard Online at
www.halleonard.com

ALL MY LOVING

VIOLIN

Words and Music by JOHN LENNON and PAUL McCARTNEY

BEAUTY AND THE BEAST

from Walt Disney's BEAUTY AND THE BEAST

Violin

Lyrics by HOWARD ASHMAN
Music by ALAN MENKEN

BLOWIN' IN THE WIND

VIOLIN

Words and Music by
BOB DYLAN

CAN YOU FEEL THE LOVE TONIGHT

from Walt Disney Pictures' THE LION KING

Violin

Music by ELTON JOHN
Lyrics by TIM RICE

CAN'T HELP FALLING IN LOVE

VIOLIN

Words and Music by GEORGE DAVID WEISS,
HUGO PERETTI and LUIGI CREATORE

CLOCKS

VIOLIN

Words and Music by GUY BERRYMAN,
JON BUCKLAND, WILL CHAMPION
and CHRIS MARTIN

DAYDREAM BELIEVER

VIOLIN

Words and Music by
JOHN STEWART

DON'T KNOW WHY

VIOLIN

Words and Music by
JESSE HARRIS

DON'T STOP BELIEVIN'

VIOLIN

Words and Music by STEVE PERRY,
NEAL SCHON and JONATHAN CAIN

EDELWEISS

from THE SOUND OF MUSIC

VIOLIN

Lyrics by OSCAR HAMMERSTEIN II
Music by RICHARD RODGERS

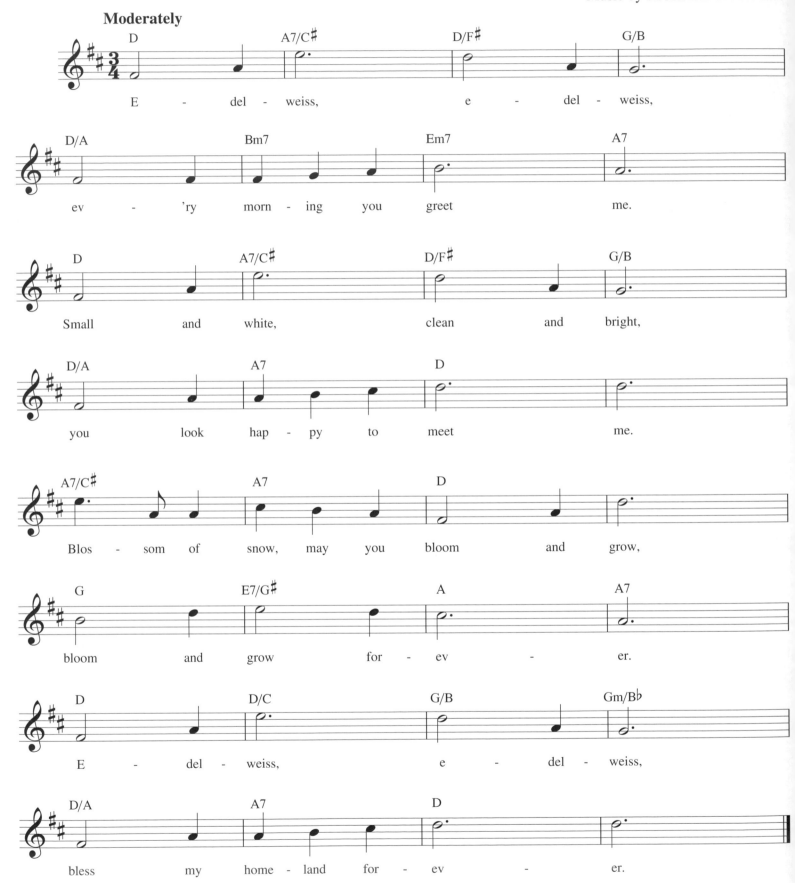

EIGHT DAYS A WEEK

VIOLIN

Words and Music by JOHN LENNON
and PAUL McCARTNEY

Moderately fast

1., 3. Ooh, I need your love, babe; guess you know it's true.
2. Love you ev - 'ry day, girl; al - ways on my mind.

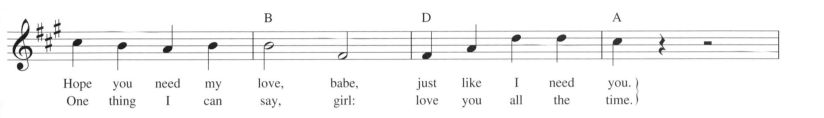

Hope you need my love, babe, just like I need you.)
One thing I can say, girl: love you all the time.)

Hold me, ___ love me, ___ hold me, ___ love me. ___

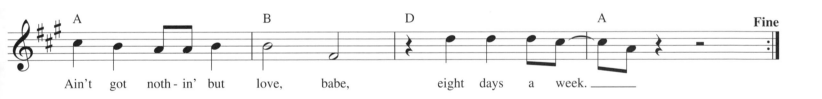

Ain't got noth - in' but love, babe, eight days a week. ___

Eight days a week I love ___ you.

Eight days a week is not e - nough to show I care. ___

EVERY BREATH YOU TAKE

VIOLIN

Music and Lyrics by
STING

Moderately

Ev-'ry breath you __ take,   ev-'ry move you __ make,
Ev-'ry move you __ make,   ev-'ry vow you __ break,

ev-'ry bond you break, ev-'ry step you take, I'll be watch-ing you.
ev-'ry smile you fake, ev-'ry claim you stake, I'll be watch-ing you.

Ev-'ry sin-gle __ day,   ev-'ry word you __ say,

ev-'ry game you play, ev-'ry night you stay, I'll be watch-ing you.

Oh, can't you __ see   you be-long to __ me?

How my poor heart __ aches __ with ev-'ry step __ you take.

D.C. al Fine

FIREFLIES

VIOLIN

Words and Music by
ADAM YOUNG

GEORGIA ON MY MIND

VIOLIN

Words by STUART GORRELL
Music by HOAGY CARMICHAEL

IN MY LIFE

Violin

Words and Music by JOHN LENNON
and PAUL McCARTNEY

HEY, SOUL SISTER

VIOLIN

Words and Music by PAT MONAHAN,
ESPEN LIND and AMUND BJORKLAND

Moderately

Hey, _____ hey, _____ hey. _____

_____ Your lip - stick stains on the front lobe of my
Just in time, I'm so glad you have a

left - side brains. I know I wouldn't for - get ya, and so I went and
one - track mind like me. You gave my life di - rec - tion, a game show love con -

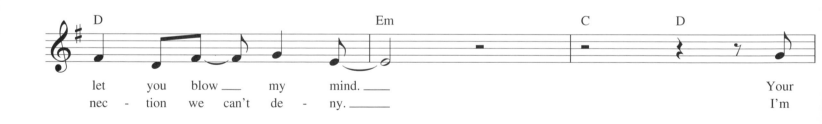

let you blow ___ my mind. ___ Your
nec - tion we can't de - ny. ___ I'm

sweet moon - beam, the smell of you in ev - 'ry sin - gle dream I dream.
so ob - sessed; my heart is bound to beat right out my un - trimmed chest. ___

_____ I knew when we col - lid - ed you're the one I have de - cid - ed   who's one of my kind. _
_____ I be - lieve in   you;   like a   vir - gin, you're Ma - don - na, and I'm   al - ways gon - na

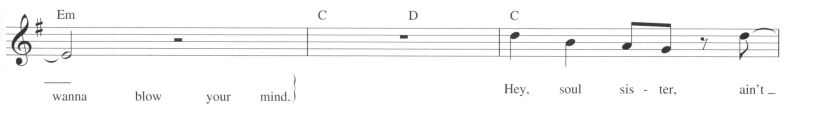

_____ wanna   blow   your   mind.)   Hey,   soul   sis - ter,   ain't _

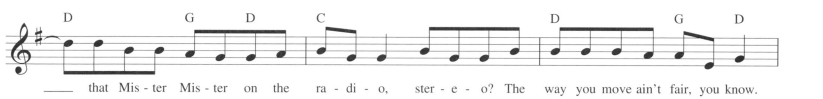

_____ that Mis - ter Mis - ter   on   the   ra - di - o,   ster - e - o? The   way you move ain't fair, you know.

Hey,   soul   sis - ter,   I _____ don't wan - na miss a sin - gle thing you do _____

_____   to - night.   Hey, _____   hey, _____

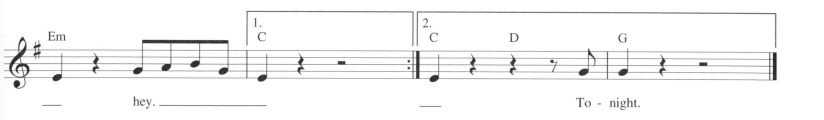

_____   hey. _____   _____   To - night.

HOT N COLD

VIOLIN

Words and Music by KATY PERRY,
MAX MARTIN and LUKASZ GOTTWALD

Moderately fast

You   change your mind ___   like a girl ___   chang-es clothes.
We   used to be ___   just like twins, ___   so in sync. ___

___   Yeah,   you   P - M - S ___   like a   girl; ___
___   The   same   en - er - gy ___   now's a   dead ___

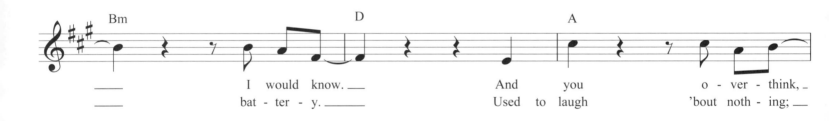

___   I   would   know. ___   And   you   o - ver - think, _
___   bat - ter - y. ___   Used   to   laugh   'bout noth - ing; ___

___   al - ways   speak ___   cryp - tic - 'ly. ___   I   should   know _
___   now you're   plain ___   bor - ing. ___   I   should   know _

___   that   you're   no   good ___   for   me. ___
___   that   you're ___   not   gon - na   change. ___

23

'Cause you're hot ____ then you're cold. You're yes ____ then you're no. You're in ____

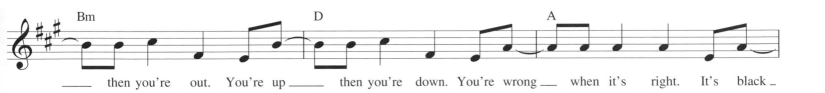

____ then you're out. You're up ____ then you're down. You're wrong ____ when it's right. It's black ____

____ and it's white. We fight, ____ we break up. We kiss, ____ we make up. ____

You don't real - ly wan - na stay, no, ____ but you don't real - ly wan - na

go. _____ You're hot ____ then you're cold. You're yes ____ then you're no. You're in ____

____ then you're out. You're up ____ then you're down. _   ____ then you're down. _

ISN'T SHE LOVELY

VIOLIN

Words and Music by
STEVIE WONDER

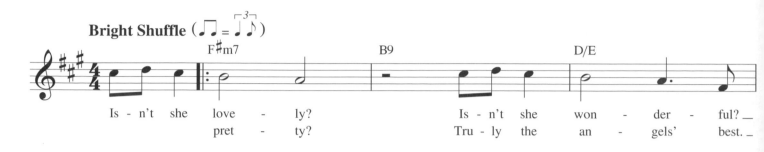

Bright Shuffle

Is - n't she love - ly? Is - n't she won - der - ful?
pret - ty? Tru - ly the an - gels' best. ___

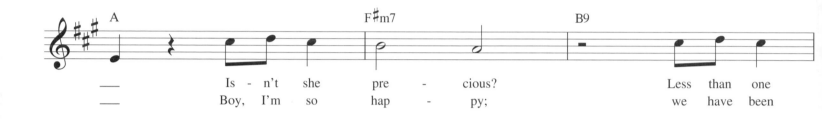

___ Is - n't she pre - cious? Less than one
___ Boy, I'm so hap - py; we have been

min - ute old. ___ I nev - er thought ___ through love we'd be ___
heav - en blessed. ___ I can't be - lieve ___ what God has done. ___

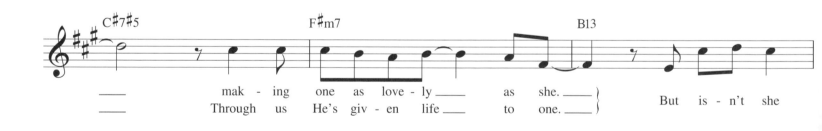

___ mak - ing one as love - ly ___ as she. ___ But is - n't she
___ Through us He's giv - en life ___ to one. ___

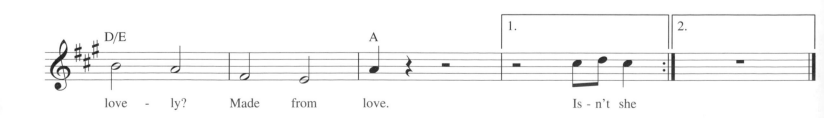

love - ly? Made from love.
1.
Is - n't she
2.

THE LETTER

Violin

Words and Music by
WAYNE CARSON THOMPSON

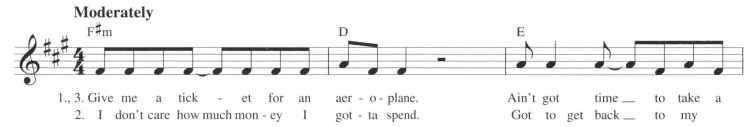

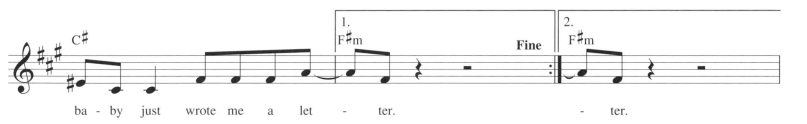

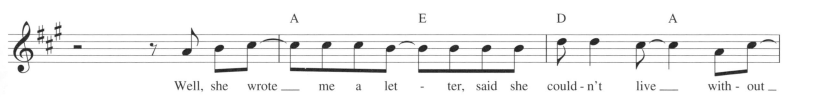

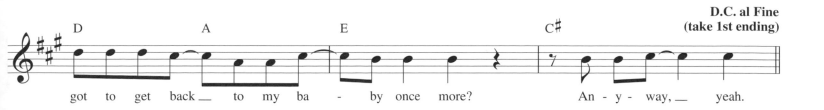

LIKE A VIRGIN

VIOLIN

Words and Music by BILLY STEINBERG
and TOM KELLY

THE LOOK OF LOVE

from CASINO ROYALE

VIOLIN

Words by HAL DAVID
Music by BURT BACHARACH

LOVE ME TENDER

VIOLIN

Words and Music by ELVIS PRESLEY
and VERA MATSON

Love me ten - der, love me sweet; nev - er let me
Love me ten - der, love me long; take me to your

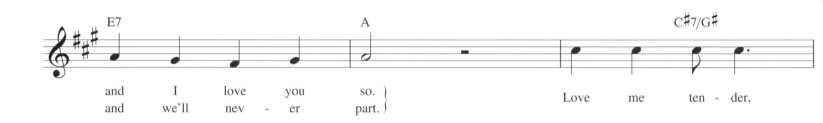

go. You have made my life com - plete,
heart. For it's there that I be - long,

and I love you so.)
and we'll nev - er part.) Love me ten - der,

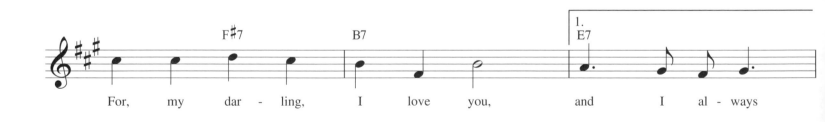

love me true. All my dreams ful - fill.

For, my dar - ling, I love you, and I al - ways

will. and I al - ways will.

MR. TAMBOURINE MAN

VIOLIN

Words and Music by
BOB DYLAN

LOVE STORY

VIOLIN

Words and Music by
TAYLOR SWIFT

Moderately

We were both young when I first saw __ you. I close my eyes __ and the

flash-back starts. _ I'm stand-ing there on a bal-co-ny in sum-mer air.

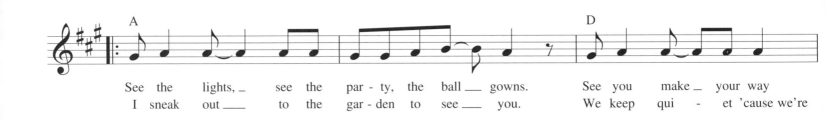

See the lights, _ see the par-ty, the ball __ gowns. See you make _ your way
I sneak out __ to the gar-den to see __ you. We keep qui - et 'cause we're

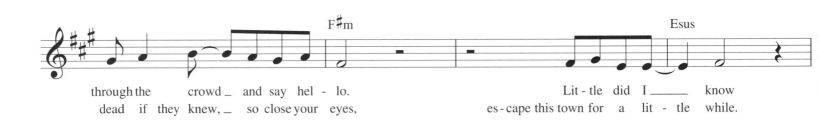

through the crowd _ and say hel - lo. Lit - tle did I _____ know
dead if they knew, _ so close your eyes, es-cape this town for a lit - tle while.

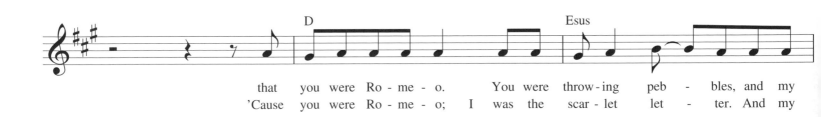

that you were Ro - me - o. You were throw-ing peb - bles, and my
'Cause you were Ro - me - o; I was the scar - let let - ter. And my

dad - dy said, "Stay a - way from Ju - li - et." __ And I was cry-ing on the stair - case,
dad - dy said, "Stay a - way from Ju - li - et." __ But you were ev - 'ry-thing to me. I was

beg - ging you, please,_ don't go. _____ And I ____ said:

Ro - me - o, take me some-where we can be a - lone. I'll be wait - ing.

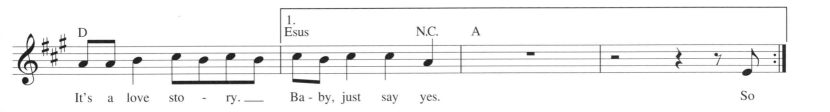

All there's left to do is run. You'll be the prince and I'll be the prin - cess.

It's a love sto - ry. ___ Ba - by, just say yes. So

Ba - by, just say ___ yes. _____ Oh, ___ oh, oh. ___

_____ Oh, ___ oh, oh, _____ oh.

'Cause we were both young when I first saw___ you. ___

MOON RIVER

from the Paramount Picture BREAKFAST AT TIFFANY'S

VIOLIN

Words by JOHNNY MERCER
Music by HENRY MANCINI

MORNING HAS BROKEN

VIOLIN

Words by ELEANOR FARJEON
Music by CAT STEVENS

MY CHERIE AMOUR

Violin

Words and Music by STEVIE WONDER,
SYLVIA MOY and HENRY COSBY

MY GIRL

Violin

Words and Music by WILLIAM "SMOKEY" ROBINSON
and RONALD WHITE

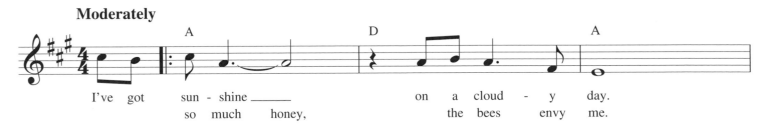

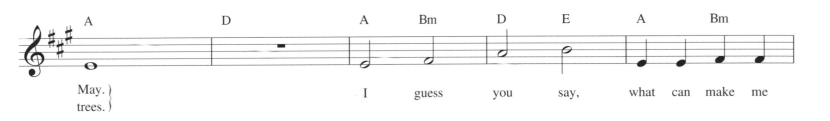

MY FAVORITE THINGS
from THE SOUND OF MUSIC

VIOLIN

Lyrics by OSCAR HAMMERSTEIN II
Music by RICHARD RODGERS

Brightly

Rain - drops on ros - es and whis - kers on kit - tens,
Cream - col - ored po - nies and crisp ap - ple stru - dels,

bright cop - per ket - tles and warm wool - en mit - tens,
door - bells and sleigh - bells and schnit - zel with noo - dles,

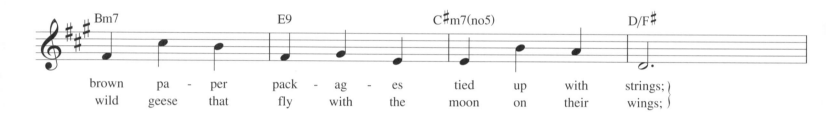

brown pa - per pack - ag - es tied up with strings;
wild geese that fly with the moon on their wings;

these are a few of my fa - vor - ite things.

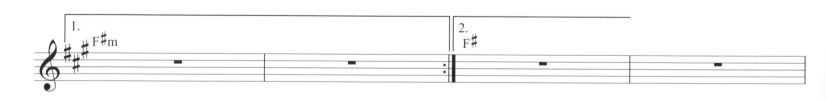

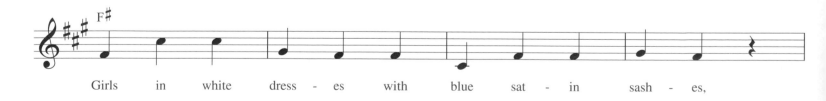

Girls in white dress - es with blue sat - in sash - es,

MY HEART WILL GO ON

(Love Theme from 'Titanic')

from the Paramount and Twentieth Century Fox Motion Picture TITANIC

VIOLIN

Music by JAMES HORNER
Lyric by WILL JENNINGS

NIGHTS IN WHITE SATIN

VIOLIN

Words and Music by
JUSTIN HAYWARD

NOWHERE MAN

VIOLIN

Words and Music by JOHN LENNON
and PAUL McCARTNEY

PUFF THE MAGIC DRAGON

VIOLIN

Words and Music by LENNY LIPTON
and PETER YARROW

RAINDROPS KEEP FALLIN' ON MY HEAD
from BUTCH CASSIDY AND THE SUNDANCE KID

Violin

Lyric by HAL DAVID
Music by BURT BACHARACH

SCARBOROUGH FAIR/CANTICLE

VIOLIN

Arrangement and Original Counter Melody by PAUL SIMON
and ARTHUR GARFUNKEL

SOMEWHERE OUT THERE
from AN AMERICAN TAIL

Violin

Music by BARRY MANN and JAMES HORNER
Lyric by CYNTHIA WEIL

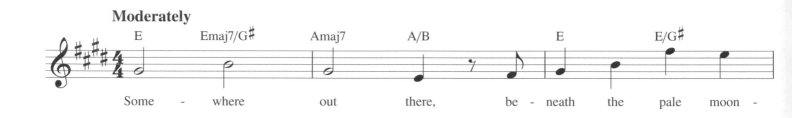

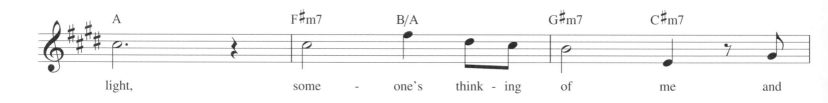

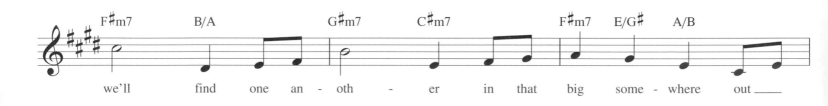

45

there.　　　　And e - ven though I know how ver - y far a - part we are, it

helps to think we might be wish - ing on the same bright star.　　And

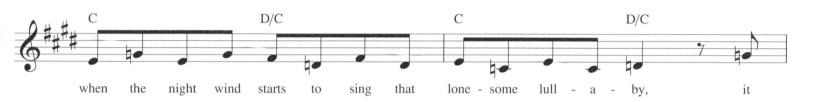

when the night wind starts to sing that lone - some lull - a - by, it

helps to think we're sleep - ing un - der - neath the same big sky.

Some - where out there, if love can see us

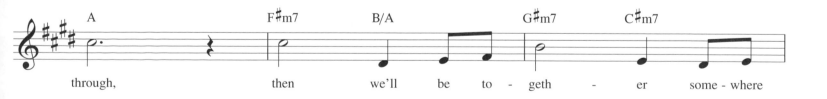

through, then we'll be to - geth - er some - where

out there, out where dreams come true.

THE SOUND OF MUSIC
from THE SOUND OF MUSIC

VIOLIN

Lyrics by OSCAR HAMMERSTEIN II
Music by RICHARD RODGERS

The hills are a-live with the sound of mu - sic, _____ with

songs they have sung for a thou - sand years. _____ The

hills fill my heart with the sound of mu - sic. _____ My

heart wants to sing ev-'ry song it hears. _____ My heart wants to

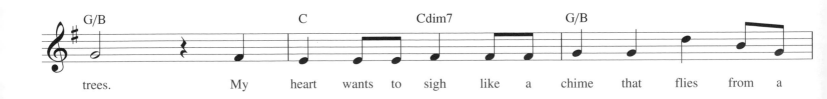

beat like the wings of the birds that rise from the lake to the

trees. My heart wants to sigh like a chime that flies from a

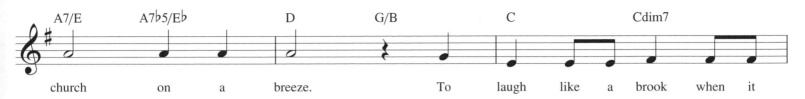

church   on   a   breeze.   To   laugh   like   a   brook   when   it

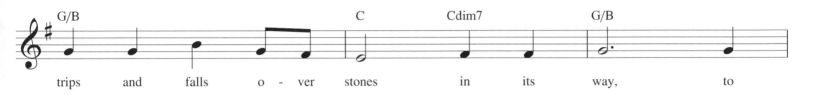

trips   and   falls   o - ver   stones   in   its   way,   to

sing   through   the   night   like   a   lark   who   is   learn - ing   to   pray.   I

go   to   the   hills   when   my   heart   is   lone - ly. _____   I

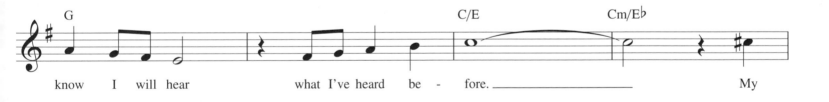

know   I   will   hear   what   I've   heard   be - fore. _____   My

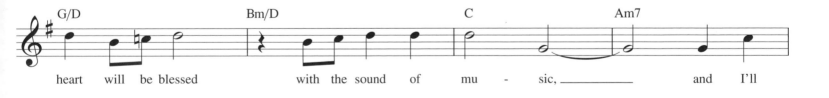

heart   will   be   blessed   with   the   sound   of   mu - sic, _____   and   I'll

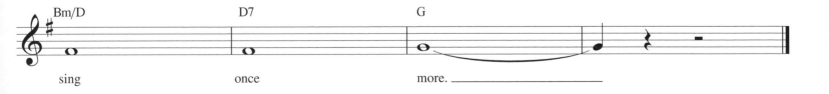

sing   once   more. _____

STRANGERS IN THE NIGHT
adapted from A MAN COULD GET KILLED

Violin

Words by CHARLES SINGLETON and EDDIE SNYDER
Music by BERT KAEMPFERT

SUNSHINE ON MY SHOULDERS

VIOLIN

Words by JOHN DENVER
Music by JOHN DENVER, MIKE TAYLOR
and DICK KNISS

SWEET CAROLINE

VIOLIN

Words and Music by
NEIL DIAMOND

Moderately

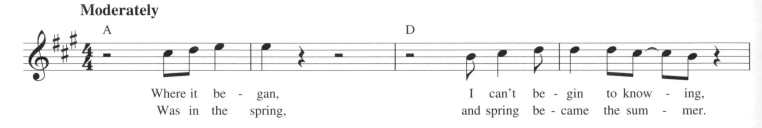

Where it be - gan,   I can't be - gin to know - ing,
Was in the spring,   and spring be - came the sum - mer.

but then, I know it's grow - ing strong.
Who'd have be - lieved you'd come __ a -

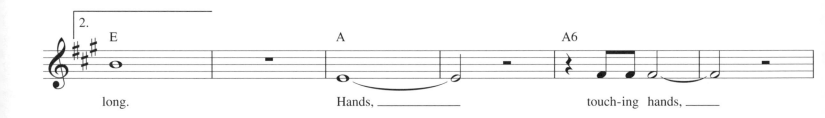

long.   Hands, _____   touch-ing hands, _____

reach-ing out,   touch-ing me,   touch-ing you. _____

Sweet Car - o - line, ____   good times nev - er seemed so
I've been in - clined ____   to be - lieve they nev - er

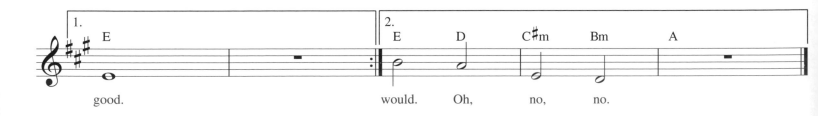

good.   would. Oh, no, no.

TILL THERE WAS YOU

from Meredith Willson's THE MUSIC MAN

Violin

By MEREDITH WILLSON

THE TIMES THEY ARE A-CHANGIN'

VIOLIN

Words and Music by
BOB DYLAN

UNCHAINED MELODY

VIOLIN

Lyric by HY ZARET
Music by ALEX NORTH

TOMORROW

from The Musical Production ANNIE

Lyric by MARTIN CHARNIN
Music by CHARLES STROUSE

Violin

Moderately fast

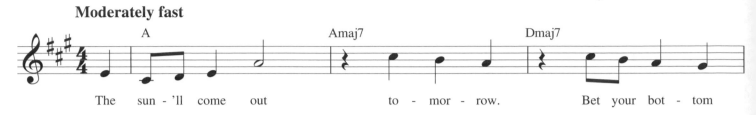

The sun-'ll come out to-mor-row. Bet your bot-tom

dol-lar that to-mor-row there'll be sun.

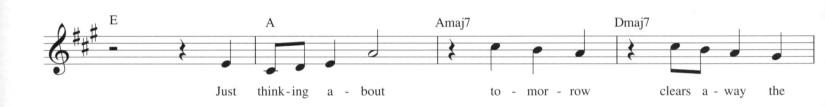

Just think-ing a-bout to-mor-row clears a-way the

cob-webs and the sor-row till there's none.

When I'm stuck with a day that's gray and lone-ly,

I just stick out my chin and grin and say, _____

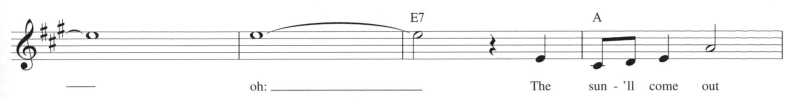

oh: _____ The sun - 'll come out

to - mor - row, so you got - ta hang on till to - mor - row,

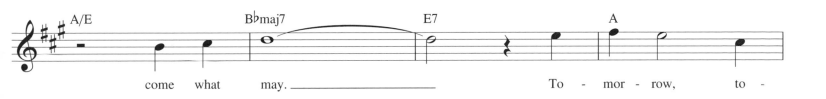

come what may. _____ To - mor - row, to -

mor - row, I love ya, to - mor - row. You're al - ways a

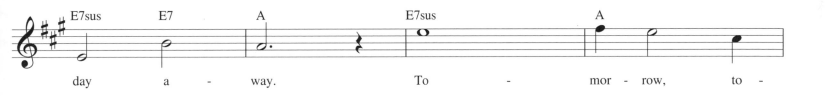

day a - way. To - mor - row, to -

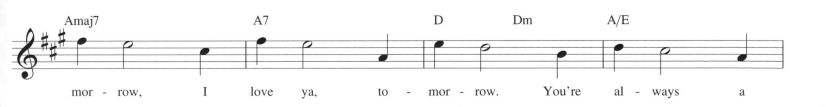

mor - row, I love ya, to - mor - row. You're al - ways a

day _____ a - way! _____

VIVA LA VIDA

VIOLIN

Words and Music by GUY BERRYMAN,
JON BUCKLAND, WILL CHAMPION
and CHRIS MARTIN

I used to rule the world. ___ Seas would rise when I gave the word. ___
___ Now in the morn-ing I sleep a - lone, ___ sweep the
streets I used to own. ___

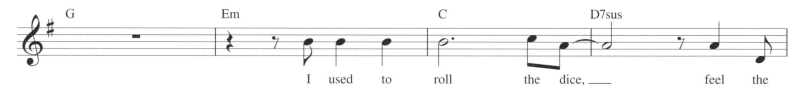

I used to roll the dice, ___ feel the

fear in my en - e - my's eyes, ___ lis - ten as the crowd ___ would sing, _

___ "Now the old king is dead; _ long live the king." One min - ute I

held the key, ___ next the walls were closed on

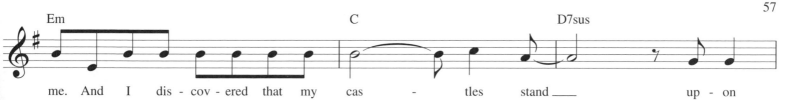

me. And I dis-cov-ered that my cas - tles stand ____ up - on

pil - lars of salt ____ and pil - lars of sand. ____ I hear Je - ru - sa - lem bells ____

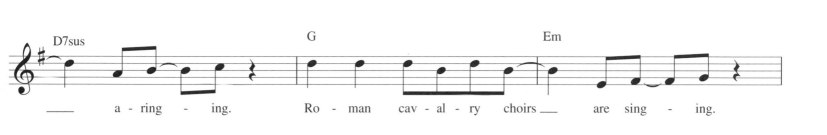

____ a - ring - ing. Ro - man cav - al - ry choirs ____ are sing - ing.

Be my mir - ror, my sword ____ and shield, ____ my mis - sion - ar - ies in a for -

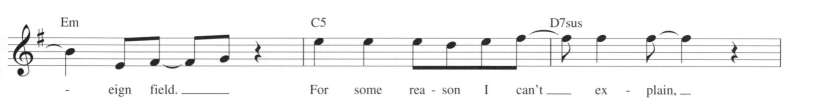

- eign field. ____ For some rea - son I can't ____ ex - plain, ____

once you've gone there was nev - er, nev - er an hon - est word, ____

____ and that was when I ruled the world. ____

WE ARE THE WORLD

VIOLIN

Words and Music by LIONEL RICHIE
and MICHAEL JACKSON

WHAT A WONDERFUL WORLD

Violin

Words and Music by GEORGE DAVID WEISS
and BOB THIELE

WONDERWALL

VIOLIN

Words and Music by
NOEL GALLAGHER

the lights _ that lead ____ us there _ are blind - ing.

There are man - y things ____ that I _____ would like to say to you, _

____ but I don't know how. _____

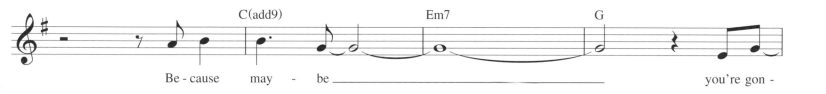

Be - cause may - be _____ you're gon -

- na be the one that saves me, _____ and

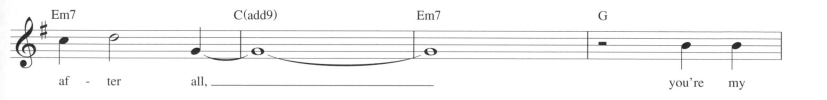

af - ter all, _____ you're my

won - der - wall. _____

YOU ARE THE SUNSHINE OF MY LIFE

VIOLIN

Words and Music by
STEVIE WONDER

You are the sun - shine of _____ my life. _____
You are the ap - ple of _____ my eye. _____

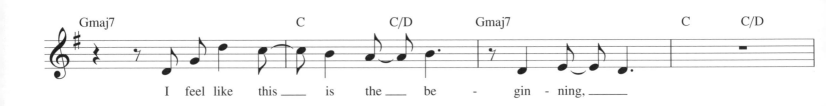

That's why I'll al - ways be _____ a - round. _____
For - ev - er you'll _____ stay in _____ my heart. _____

I feel like this _____ is the _____ be - gin - ning, _____

though I've loved you _____ for a thou - sand years. _____

And if I thought _____ our love _____ was end - ing, _____ I'd find _____

_____ my - self _____ drown - ing in my _____ own tears. Whoa, _____ whoa. _____

YOU'VE GOT A FRIEND

VIOLIN

Words and Music by
CAROLE KING

HAL•LEONARD

Audio Access Included

EASY INSTRUMENTAL PLAY-ALONG

- Perfect for beginning players
- Carefully edited to include only the notes and rhythms that students learn in the first months playing their instrument

- Great-sounding demonstration and play-along tracks
- Audio tracks can be accessed online for download or streaming, using the unique code inside the book

DISNEY
Book with Online Audio Tracks

The Ballad of Davy Crockett • Can You Feel the Love Tonight • Candle on the Water • I Just Can't Wait to Be King • The Medallion Calls • Mickey Mouse March • Part of Your World • Whistle While You Work • You Can Fly! You Can Fly! You Can Fly! • You'll Be in My Heart (Pop Version).

00122184	Flute	$9.99
00122185	Clarinet	$9.99
00122186	Alto Sax	$9.99
00122187	Tenor Sax	$9.99
00122188	Trumpet	$9.99
00122189	Horn	$9.99
00122190	Trombone	$9.99
00122191	Violin	$9.99
00122192	Viola	$9.99
00122193	Cello	$9.99
00122194	Keyboard Percussion	$9.99

CLASSIC ROCK
Book with Online Audio Tracks

Another One Bites the Dust • Born to Be Wild • Brown Eyed Girl • Dust in the Wind • Every Breath You Take • Fly like an Eagle • I Heard It Through the Grapevine • I Shot the Sheriff • Oye Como Va • Up Around the Bend.

00122195	Flute	$9.99
00122196	Clarinet	$9.99
00122197	Alto Sax	$9.99
00122198	Tenor Sax	$9.99
00122201	Trumpet	$9.99
00122202	Horn	$9.99
00122203	Trombone	$9.99
00122205	Violin	$9.99
00122206	Viola	$9.99
00122207	Cello	$9.99
00122208	Keyboard Percussion	$9.99

CLASSICAL THEMES
Book with Online Audio Tracks

Can Can • Carnival of Venice • Finlandia • Largo from Symphony No. 9 ("New World") • Morning • Musette in D Major • Ode to Joy • Spring • Symphony No. 1 in C Minor, Fourth Movement Excerpt • Trumpet Voluntary.

00123108	Flute	$9.99
00123109	Clarinet	$9.99
00123110	Alto Sax	$9.99
00123111	Tenor Sax	$9.99
00123112	Trumpet	$9.99
00123113	Horn	$9.99
00123114	Trombone	$9.99
00123115	Violin	$9.99
00123116	Viola	$9.99
00123117	Cello	$9.99
00123118	Keyboard Percussion	$9.99

CHRISTMAS CAROLS
Book with Online Audio Tracks

Angels We Have Heard on High • Christ Was Born on Christmas Day • Come, All Ye Shepherds • Come, Thou Long-Expected Jesus • Good Christian Men, Rejoice • Jingle Bells • Jolly Old St. Nicholas • Lo, How a Rose E'er Blooming • On Christmas Night • Up on the Housetop.

00130363	Flute	$9.99
00130364	Clarinet	$9.99
00130365	Alto Sax	$9.99
00130366	Tenor Sax	$9.99
00130367	Trumpet	$9.99
00130368	Horn	$9.99
00130369	Trombone	$9.99
00130370	Violin	$9.99
00130371	Viola	$9.99
00130372	Cello	$9.99
00130373	Keyboard Percussion	$9.99

POP FAVORITES
Book with Online Audio Tracks

Achy Breaky Heart (Don't Tell My Heart) • I'm a Believer • Imagine • Jailhouse Rock • La Bamba • Louie, Louie • Ob-La-Di, Ob-La-Da • Splish Splash • Stand by Me • Yellow Submarine.

00232231	Flute	$9.99
00232232	Clarinet	$9.99
00232233	Alto Sax	$9.99
00232234	Tenor Sax	$9.99
00232235	Trumpet	$9.99
00232236	Horn	$9.99
00232237	Trombone	$9.99
00232238	Violin	$9.99
00232239	Viola	$9.99
00232240	Cello	$9.99
00233296	Keyboard Percussion	$9.99

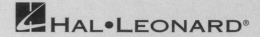

HAL•LEONARD®

www.halleonard.com

Prices, content, and availability subject to change without notice.